Using Information and Communication Technology

Cross-curricular Internet Projects

A Teacher's Resource Book of Photocopiable Worksheets

Maldwyn Pryse and Claire Allen

Contents

Teacher's notes

Introduction

Using Information and Communication Technology - Cross-curricular Internet Projects is a resource book of photocopiable worksheets to develop pupils' Information and Communication Technology skills across the curriculum using the educational potential of the Internet. Greater emphasis is being placed on sharing information between schools and this is reflected in the email / IECC (Intercultural E-mail Classroom Connections) projects (see page 5 and Worksheet 15) suggested in the book. Short, focused tasks are seen as a practical means of using ICT in a classroom situation and the cross-curricular nature of the projects ensures that ICT is an integral part of the curriculum – thus meeting the new inspection framework requirements.

Organisation

The worksheets can be used in their entirety or in part according to the time available and/or the ICT skills of the pupils. In the majority of cases it is expected that teachers will introduce each activity and discuss the main teaching points before pupils begin working.

Pupils can work individually, at a computer, to complete activities, but it is often beneficial for them to work with a partner. By working in collaboration with others, pupils are able to discuss and refine their ideas further. Additionally, by approaching the activities in a shared way, pupils learn to co-operate with each other. Care should be taken, however, to ensure that one pupil doesn't dominate the activity to the detriment of the other. The importance of the role of helper should be emphasised to pupils, in addition to the importance of hands-on work, when introducing activities.

It is often advantageous to allow pupils who are more confident with the computer to attempt the activity first. These pupils can then help the subsequent pupils, who can then in turn help others. This chain effect of pupils helping each other helps to reinforce learning, frees the teacher and enables peer teaching.

Web sites

Due to the nature of the Internet we cannot guarantee that the sites mentioned will always be available. However, a latest possible list is to be found on the Evans Brothers Ltd web site:

www.evansbooks.co.uk

All of the activities require the use of the Internet and some encourage the use of email. Creating favourites folders helps to organise projects or pupils' most useful web sites efficiently online. Click and hold ***Favourites***, a drop down menu will appear, release the mouse button over ***Organise Favourites***. Click on the new folder icon. Type in a name over the highlighted text - this could be the pupil's name or the name of a project. Press return. You have now created a new favourites folder. ***Close*** the organise favourites window. Click and hold ***Favourites***, your new folder should now appear in the list. When you want to save work to a folder, go to ***Favourites*** then ***Add Favourite***. Click ***Create In***, select the appropriate folder and the site you are currently visiting will be filed here for quick and easy access.

School policy on the use of the Internet

Before using the projects we strongly advise teachers to consider the following questions:

- Does the school have an acceptable use policy (AUP) for using the internet?
- Does the policy require parents to sign a consent form?
- Has guidance been sought from the LEA on development of the policy?
- Does the school access the Internet via a proxy server or 'walled garden provider' which censors unsuitable material?
- Does the school have strategies for dealing with undesirable material?
- What arrangements are made for supervision of pupils whilst using the Internet?

Information regarding the above issues can be found as part of an information sheet prepared by BECTa, "The Internet and the World Wide Web", or on their web site

www.becta.org.uk

Please ensure that pupils type web site addresses accurately as some unsuitable sites are choosing common misspellings as their address to increase the number of visitors to their site.

Software

The activities in this booklet do not specify the software required to complete them or specify which browser to use in order to view the web pages. It is expected that a range of software packages will be used. The following types of programs will be required: a web browser, a word processing program, a desktop publishing package (DTP), a graphics/drawing package, a database program and a spreadsheet program.

Word processing

Word processing involves entering text via a keyboard using a word processing program. A range of word processing programs is available today for use in schools. Word processing is popular as it makes writing an easier and less frustrating activity. Pupils who usually find writing a chore are often motivated by the impressive results which they can achieve by using a word processor.

The appearance of text can be changed when using a word processor. It can be enlarged or reduced in size, and the style and colour can also be altered to give interesting results.

Desk-top publishing

Desk-top publishing programs are particularly good to use when producing newspapers, newsletters and advertisements. They are good because they allow pictures and text to be inserted into boxes (frames). These boxes can then be moved around the page. Additionally, the boxes can be made bigger or smaller and given borders. Examples of popular desk-top publishing programs are Microsoft's 'Publisher' and Softease's Multimedia textease.

Drawing programs

There are a number of programs that will allow the user to draw and design pictures. Images can usually be drawn freely using different brush types and straight lines can be created with a variety of line thicknesses. Colours are usually selected from a palette. Some programs allow the user to stamp on a selection of ready-drawn pictures without leaving the program.

Database programs

A database program allows the user to store data in a structured way. The information in a database can be searched and sorted so that specific data can be located quickly and efficiently, thus assisting them with the process of finding things out. Databases are usually used to store, amend, present and retrieve information whilst enabling pupils to develop ideas. In using databases accessed on the Internet pupils are extending their skills by accessing remote data and interrogating it for a specific purpose.

In the databases suggested in these materials, data is entered under headings called "fields". A database entitled "Houses" might include the following field headings: Address, Type, No. of bedrooms, Garage, Central Heating, Double Glazing, En-suite, Cost. There are three types of field structure: alphabetic fields, numeric fields and alphanumeric fields. Alphabetic fields recognise letters, numeric fields recognise numbers and alphanumeric fields recognise both. When setting up fields, the type of field will normally need to be identified as this can have an effect on the type of graphs that can be generated. Once the fields have been established, data can be entered. Each "page" of information entered is called a "record".

Address	Ocean View
Type	Detached
No of bedrooms	5
Garage	Yes
Central Heating	Yes
Double Glazing	Yes
En-suite	No
Cost	£125,000

a record

Once information has been stored in a database, records can be sorted and searched. Fields can be sorted numerically into ascending or descending order (e.g. most expensive house and least expensive house) or alphabetically. Specific information can be searched e.g. how many bedrooms are there in Ocean View? Searches for information can also be made using more than one criterion e.g. how many detached houses are there which cost more than (>) £120,000?

Information that has been entered into a database can be printed out record by record or in sorted lists. Many programs also allow the information to be presented as graphs.

The use of email allows pupils to share information such as datafiles and this can greatly enrich their educational experiences and foster further collaborative work – whether with a school within the same LEA or on another continent!

Examples of popular database programs would be Black Cat's First Workshop or Black Cat and RM's "Information Workshop".

Spreadsheets

A spreadsheet is a type of program which allows data to be stored and manipulated. The spreadsheet looks like a grid and is made up of rows and columns. Each individual position on a spreadsheet is called a cell. A cell can be identified by selecting the column it is in and the row it is in. The columns are located by letters, the rows by numbers. For example, cell B2 is highlighted below:

	A	B	C	D
1				
2		B2		
3				

Numbers can be entered into cells. Calculations can take place on those numbers by inserting simple formulae. After entering formulae, calculations are

automatically performed. For example, when multiplying the number 6 in cell A1, by the number 3 in cell B1, a formula could be inserted in cell C1. After entering the formula the answer will automatically appear in cell C1. An example of a formula in this case is:
=A1*B1 (computers use * as the multiplication sign).

	A	B	C
1	6	3	=A1*B1
2			
3			

Teachers will need to refer to the software manuals of the spreadsheet package they are using for details of formulae that can be used with a particular program.

Text can also be entered on to a spreadsheet. This usually helps to explain what the numbers mean. Sometimes, when inserting text or formulae, the columns will need to be widened and this can usually be done by moving the cursor to the edge of the column and dragging with the mouse. If one column needs to be narrower than the others you can also distribute the remaining columns or rows evenly. You can also set the cell height and width or use auto fit as the case may be.

Spreadsheets can be used to present a wide variety of information. The real value of using a spreadsheet, however, is that once a spreadsheet has been completed, should any change be made to numeric values or formulae, the effects of the changes upon the rest of the spreadsheet are immediately displayed. Examples of popular primary spreadsheet packages are Research Machine's Starting Grid, Microsoft's Excel and Black Cat's Number Box.

A variety of graphs can be constructed by using the graphics facility of a spreadsheet. A bar chart, pie chart or line graph is usually constructed by entering columns of data on to a spreadsheet grid, highlighting them and then clicking on a chart tool button, icon or word.

Using spreadsheets enables pupils to develop ideas, to investigate the effect of changing values and to identify patterns and relationships.

As with databases, the use of email allows pupils to share information and research data with other schools. In doing so they can expand on their experiments or problem-solving work and share their findings with pupils around the world. They could also plan an experiment from the outset with another class of pupils, share and present their results e.g. a shadow project (see Worksheet 15).

Assessment

Most of the activities in this book require pupils to save their work and to provide either written or printed evidence of their work. A pupil's record sheet is provided which can be copied and completed by each pupil for each activity. In addition to examining recorded/saved evidence of pupils' work, we strongly encourage teachers to observe and question pupils working at a computer, in order to assess their levels of confidence. It is recommended that pupils are given a folder and disk/s in order to store their work.

Printing

Children should be taught to use printing resources carefully. Web pages can be printed by clicking on ***File*** followed by ***Print*** or on the printer icon on the Tool bar. Almost all of the activities that require the use of a printer can be completed using a black and white printer. A colour printer may give more impressive results for some of the activities, however.

Saving

It is assumed that teachers will be able to show their pupils how to save within software packages normally used within the classroom. However it is worth noting that pupils in Key Stage 2 are expected to be able to save work independently of the teacher as a requirement of achieving Level 3.

Saving text from a web page

a) Copy the text and paste it into a word processor as follows:
Highlight all the text, press Ctrl + C or click on ***Edit*** followed by ***Copy***, minimise the web browser using the minus type icon in the top right hand corner of the screen, open a new page on your word processing package, press Ctrl + V or click on ***Edit*** followed by ***Paste***, read the contents of the web page on your word processing package and save as you would any other piece of work.
b) Save the web page directly as a text file as follows:
Click on ***File***, followed by ***Save As***. A new window appears on screen. Click on the black arrow head near the ***Save in*** window and choose where you want to save your work e.g. ***3½ Floppy A***. You also need to set the ***Save as type*** window to ***Text File (.txt)*** by clicking on the black arrow-head and giving the file a meaningful name.

Saving graphics from a web page

a) Save the graphic directly as a bitmap file as follows:
Click on the graphic you want to save using the **RIGHT** hand mouse button. A new window appears on screen. Click on ***Save Picture As***. Another new window appears on the screen. Click on the black arrow-head near the ***Save in*** window and choose where you want to save your work e.g. ***3½ Floppy A***. You also need to set the ***Save as type*** window to ***Bitmap (*.BMP)*** if working within a Windows environment and you need to use Paint.

b) Copy the graphic and paste into a word processor, DTP or graphics package as follows:
You can also click on the graphic you want to save by using the **RIGHT** hand mouse button and click on ***Copy*** using your left hand mouse button. The graphic is copied and can be ***pasted*** into most word processing or DTP packages. The graphic could also be ***pasted*** into your graphics package e.g. RM's Colour Magic, and manipulated.

(If you really like the graphic you could also click the **RIGHT** hand mouse button on the graphic and click on ***Set as Wallpaper***.)

Search engines

Much has been written on this issue including the information sheet published by BECTa in February 1999, "Internet Searching". Visit their web site for a free copy!

www.becta.org.uk

You could also try the following site:

http://daphne.palomar.edu/TGSEARCH/

Setting up international email and/or projects

Sharing and exchanging information will grow in importance within ICT with the onset of NGfL (the National Grid for Learning). The Intercultural E-Mail Classroom Connections is a FREE service to help teachers link with partners in other countries and cultures for email classroom key-pal (NOT pen-pal!) and project exchanges. During a recent visit to their web site

www.iecc.org

it was noted that more than 7,200 teachers in 79 countries were participating in one or more of the IECC lists.

The sections of the web site of most use to the primary school are:
IECC (for K-12) which is intended for teachers seeking partner classrooms for international and cross-cultural email exchanges. Consider browsing postings to this section or subscribing (free!) in order to receive mailings. You might find a school looking for partner schools in the UK on a subject/theme that you are involved in – remember there is no guarantee that they will respond to your reply, although most do.
IECC – **Projects** is an electronic mailing list where teachers may announce or request help with specific classroom projects that involve email, internationally or cross-culturally. After gaining experience using IECC (for K-12) this section places YOU in the driving seat, requesting others to join your project e.g. weather exchange, shadow exchange etc.

Without doubt, effective use of email has enormous educational potential. The enthusiasm generated by collaborative, interactive email projects is real and can reap benefits.
Other web pages that could help you find partners are:

www.wotw.org.uk
www.bc.org.au/montage

QCA Curriculum Review

During the writing of this book the QCA published its review of the National Curriculum which included a new Programme of Study for ICT. The proposed new Programme of Study uses new terminology. Skills, knowledge and understanding now includes Finding things out; Developing ideas and making things happen; Sharing information; and Reviewing, modifying and evaluating work as it progresses.

Key to worksheet symbols

S	Save	P	Print
D	Download		

ICT across the curriculum

	Literacy	Numeracy	Science	ICT	History	Geography	Music	Art	D+T	RE
Read all about it	■	■		■					■	
A quick search	■	■		■					■	
Egyptian Writing	■			■	■					
Castles	■			■	■				■	
What's that bird?	■	■	■	■						
Battle Abbey	■			■	■				■	■
Your local area	■			■		■				
House search	■	■		■		■				
Volcanoes	■		■	■		■			■	
We're off!	■	■		■	■	■				
Finding out about whales	■		■	■						
Is this me?	■			■						
The weather	■	■		■		■		■		
The *Titanic*	■			■	■			■		
Email a shadow	■	■	■	■		■				
Religions of the world	■		■	■			■			■
Where do you live?	■	■		■		■				
Car search	■	■		■		■				
Party time	■	■		■					■	
An assembly	■		■	■	■	■	■	■		■
Dinosaur data	■	■		■	■	■				
What's their web site like?	■			■			■		■	
Create a school web page	■			■					■	
CD-ROMs	■	■		■						

1 Read all about it!

Name ______________________

Write an article for your own class 'national' newspaper.

Choose one from the following article headings. It may be a good idea to work in pairs.

Foreign News **Home Affairs** **Sport** **Fashion** **T.V. Critic**

Using reports from the national papers, write your own simplified article from the facts you have found. Use the following web sites to help you.

www.newsday.co.uk/index.html

www.pa.press.net

http://news.bbc.co.uk

http://express.lineone.net

www.the-times.co uk

www.totalwales.com

www.independent.co.uk

www.guardian.co.uk

Use a word-processing package to write up your article.

Tip: Newspapers use a font called 'Times New Roman'.
Use this font to give your words a real newspaper look!

Read all about it!

Try to predict what the main stories will be in tomorrow's papers.
Use the web sites to check if you were right!

S P Use a DTP package to design and create a class newspaper from all the articles created by the pupils. Print out your work.

If you were paid at a rate of 27p per word,
how much would you have earned for your article? . . . .

Tip: To find the number of words, click on ***File***, on ***Properties*** and choose ***Statistics***.

Why not set up a spreadsheet to calculate the amount?

How much more would you receive if you had 32p per word? . . . .

How much less would you receive if you had 21p per word? . . . .

How much more would you receive if you had a 12.5% rise? . . . .

Browse . . .

2 A quick search

Name

You are starting up in business as a driving instructor and are hoping to set up your own driving school. You need to find out how many other driving schools there are in your area.

Look at the following web site:

www.yell.co.uk

Tip: Conduct a search using the words *driving school*.

The printed Yellow Pages directory can be the *quickest* way of finding information like this and the web site will provide the *most up-to-date* information.

Was it easier to search using the printed Yellow Pages than the Internet version?

Extension work:
Look at the Yellow Pages directory, and see which of the driving school adverts attracts you the most.

How can you advertise your business to attract customers?
What things can you offer that the other driving schools don't?

S P Design your own advert, to promote your driving school, offering special help for young drivers. Save and print your work.

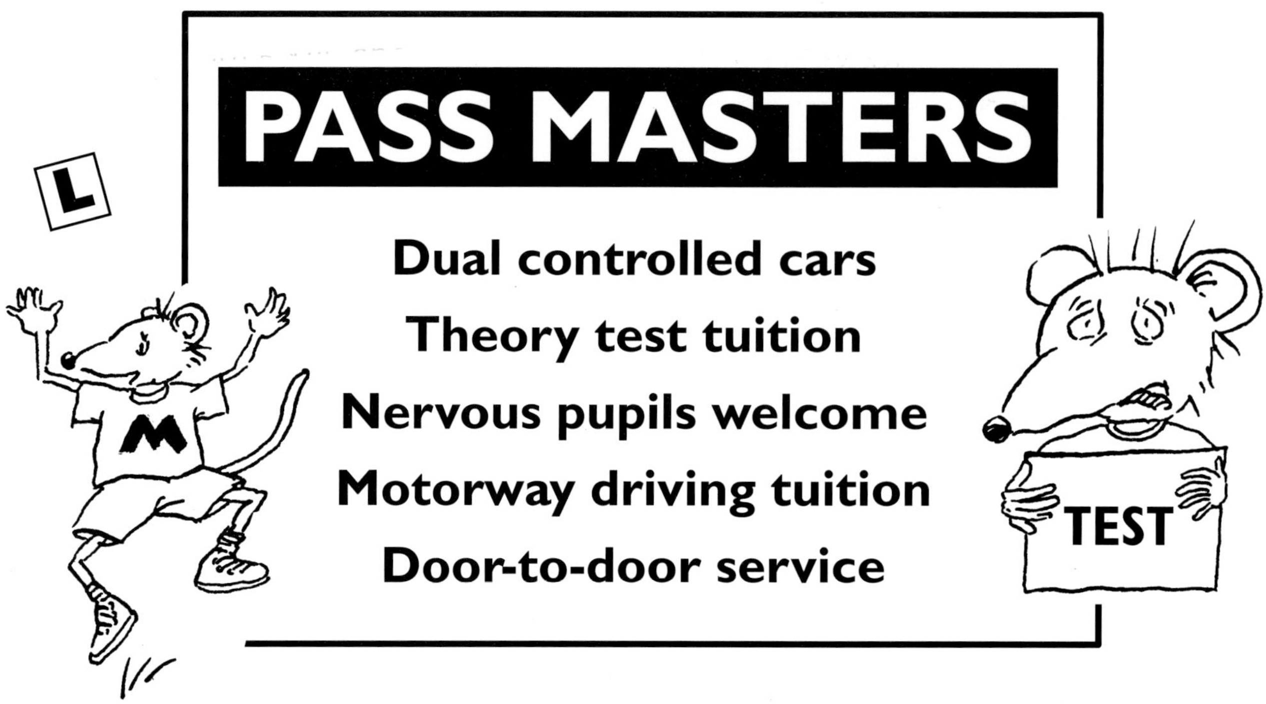

3

Egyptian writing

Name ____________________

You can see three pictures of birds. These pictures form part of the Egyptian alphabet. Can you find out which letters they represent? You can find the information by looking at the following web site:

http://eyelid.ukonline.co.uk/ancient/hiero1.htm

The pictures that make up the alphabet are called hieroglyphics and were a very sophisticated form of communication.

1. See if you can find the pictures that spell your name. You can use the links on the web site to research the task.
2. Find the letters that spell a word, perhaps a friend's name. Copy the pictures as carefully as you can, and ask them what the word is! You can translate it for them.
3. Think of a message and use the pictures as a code. Ask a friend to decipher it. Your friend must think of a message to write back, using hieroglyphics. Did you decipher the message?

Browse . . .

Castles

Name

Castles were not only places for the rich and powerful. Soldiers, cooks and servants also lived within the castle. Can you think of others who lived in the castle?

Imagine you are a 'commoner' living in the castle.
Choose the type of work you do and describe your day.

Think about the time you would have to get up
to perform your duties, the time when you go to bed.
What would you eat during the day?
What clothes would you wear?

Find the information you might need on the following web site:

www.castles-of-britain.com

Tip: Click on the ***Castle Learning Centre*** and choose the relevant sections.

Other useful sites:

www.castlewales.com/life.html
www.castlesontheweb.com

D S Don't forget to download and save any pictures you want to illustrate your work.

Extension work:
You have been given the task of designing a new castle. Follow the task as set in

http://score.rims.k12.ca.us/activity/castlebuild.html

Follow the links on this web page – they might help you with the first task on this page!

What's that bird?

Name ______________________

How much do you know about the birds in your locality? Which birds can you identify?

At different times of the year the varieties of birds to be seen can vary. Do you know which birds can be seen during January and February or during May and June?

Using the RSPB web site

www.rspb.org.uk

make a list of birds and other wildlife which can be seen at the two different times of the year.

Keep a diary, using a word processor, of birds seen in your locality during the year. Do some of them match those suggested on the RSPB site?

Tip: Click on ***Under 18? Follow Me***, click on the ***YOC Bird Life*** icon on the top of the page (banner) followed by ***Other Stories - Get Out Now*** and finally choose the section you wish to read.

Extension work:
Follow some of the other links on the RSPB site:
Under 18? Follow me, ***Projects – Kestrels*** or ***Red for danger*** or ***Seashore Explorer***.

It would be ideal if you could visit a web site which could help you identify birds using an on-line database. You could use a search engine named *Ask Jeeves for kids* to help you

www.ajkids.com/

Once you've found the site type: *Where can I find a bird identification web site?* Click on the USA map icon for the OnLine Bird Identification Guide. Find pictures of a golden eagle. Compare these with the information found on the RSPB site ***Bird Life*** – ***Other Stories*** – ***Bird File*** – ***Golden Wonder***.

Write an email to the RSPB asking if they know of any pages on the web which could help you identify birds in your locality.

6

Battle Abbey

Name

You have probably heard about the Battle of Hastings, but the Abbey at the village of Battle also has a fascinating history. From the following web site write a mini-project on 'Battle Abbey'.

www.castlesontheweb.com

Do a search using the word ***Abbey***. You will find several pages. Look for the ***Village of Battle*** and one on ***Battle Abbey***. Both are useful to look at for the background information you will need.

S P Use a word-processing or DTP package to write, save and present your work. Use a multimedia package to present your information, for example Textease.

Browse . . .

Your local area

Name

Where do you live? In the countryside? In a town? In a village?

Make a list of the advantages and disadvantages of living in your area.

Contact another school in an area that is different from yours. Ask the pupils there to make their own list of the advantages and disadvantages of living in their area. Compare the two lists. What would YOU like about living where they do? What would you not like about living there?

You can find a contrasting school by searching the following web site:

www.iecc.org

Use email to ask them about their area. You can also send them YOUR information, and ask them what they would like and dislike about where you live.

You could construct a more detailed questionnaire, and involve parents with questions such as:

1 Where do they work?

2 What is the main industry?

3 How far do they travel to work?

4 Do they shop locally or at an out-of-town superstore?

Find out as much as you can, and ask your partner school to send photographs of their area, in order to make a wall display showing all the contrasts you have found. (Pictures could be sent by post or as files attached to the emails.)

Browse . . .

House search

Name

Your parents are looking for a new house to purchase. They would like a four-bedroom detached house with a garage and garden with as many modern conveniences as possible, in any part of the country.

Use a search engine such as 'Yahoo' or 'Alta Vista' to help you with your search:

www.altavista.com www.yahoo.com

To search for a specific area you could use the following UK-based search engines to help you:

www.ukdirectory.co.uk www.yell.co.uk

and look under **Estate Agents**.

Tip: Try using the following search technique to ensure accurate results: estate + agents + (your area/town name)

Search for:

1 the cheapest **2** the dearest

3 the nearest **4** the one you really like

Compare using online estate agents and published lists from estate agents. What are the advantages and disadvantages of both?

Use the above web sites to choose 15 houses priced between £50,000 and £150,000. Record your results in a database using the following fields:

Address Type Bedrooms Garage Central heating Double glazing En-suite Cost

Print your work. Do you notice any trends in prices? Are similar houses the same price around the country? Can you give reasons for your answer?

Location	Dinas Powys, Cardiff
Type	Semi-detached
Bedrooms	3
Garage	Yes
Central Heating	Gas
Double Glazing	No
En-suite	No
Cost	£74,950

Maidstone, Kent
Semi-detatched
3
Yes
Yes
Yes
No
£128.000

Browse . . .

Volcanoes

Name

Choose a title from the following list and prepare a short project on volcanoes. It should be written for younger children. When you have finished your project make a short presentation to a class younger than you and tell them, in a way they can understand, all you have found out.

The Italian volcanoes
Erupting volcanoes
Myths and legends surrounding volcanoes

You can find information and pictures on the following web site:

http://volcano.und.nodak.edu

Don't forget, you can use a search engine to search the Internet for another volcano site.

To illustrate your talk, you can make a backdrop of a huge fiery picture of a volcano. Even better, you could build your own model of an erupting volcano. Visit the following web site and follow the simple instructions:

http://onlinebiz.com/zach/mvols.htm

You can also tell younger pupils how you have found the information and give them some tips on how to find the information for themselves!

Extension work:
Prepare a news bulletin on a current eruption using Volcano World. Click on ***Teaching and Learning*** followed by ***On Line Education Programme***, ***Volcano World On Line Lessons***, ***VOLC News***.

Tip: When searching for information in Volcano World you can find some of the information needed for your presentation by clicking on ***World Region*** followed by ***Europe/West Asia***. Remember using the ***Search For*** option at the bottom of the page can also save time e.g. searching for myths and legends. Interesting and fun material can also be found by clicking on ***Kid's Door*** – it's well worth a visit!

Browse . . .

10 We're off!

Name ______________________________

Your school is going on an overnight history trip to either London, Cardiff or Edinburgh. You have to plan the trip.

Find out the train times from the station nearest your school. If you have to change trains, you need to make a note of the times and where you change trains. You need to find out what time the train arrives at its destination.

You also need to know the times of the return journey.

Find the information you need from the following web sites:

www.a2btravel.co.uk
http://bahn.hafas.de/english.html

Do a search for the tourist board in the city. Find the best/cheapest accommodation where you can stay for one night. What historical sights could you visit?

Type your findings in the form of an information sheet for parents and include an itinerary.

What other information might be useful for parents to know? Think about contact telephone numbers, and whether you will need packed lunches or stop at cafés – it's your trip, it's up to you!

Browse . . .

11 Finding out about whales

Name ____________________

How much do you know about whales? Do whales eat fish? Do whales lay eggs like fish? Are whales fish?

From the web site www.tictoc.co.uk try to find out the answers to the following questions.

1. What is the reason there are so few whales living in our oceans?

   ....

2. What is a 'baleen' whale?

   ....

3. Name a toothed whale.

   ....

4. Where does the beluga whale live?

   ....

5. What is so special about the narwhal?

   ....

6. How do whales communicate?

   ....

7. Which whale is the largest?

   ....

8. How do whales breathe?

   ....

9. In which oceans would you find whales?

   ....

10. What is a baby whale known as?

   ....

You could choose one of the tasks shown on the site and learn a bit more about these wonderful creatures.

Browse . . .

12 Is this me?

Name

What do you look like? Is your hair short or long? Have you a round shaped face or an oval shaped face? Is your nose pointed or snubbed? Have you fair hair or dark? Could you draw a picture of yourself?

Many artists have done 'self portraits'. One of the most famous artists is Vincent Van Gogh. Go to the following web site and study some of his self portraits.

www.vangoghgallery.com/

When you get to the site, scroll down until you find **categories** and then click on **self portraits**

How has he painted them? Do you think he has represented himself honestly?

Try to draw a self portrait. Use a mirror to check how your hair falls round your face, how large your eyes are, etc.

Don't show your portrait to anyone else. Get your teacher to collect all the drawings and show them to the class. Can you correctly identify each portrait?

You could look at some of Van Gogh's other paintings such as 'Starry night' or 'Sunflowers' and see if you can paint the same picture.

For examples of self portraits by other artists why not visit:

www.nationalgallery.org.uk
www.southern.net/wm/

Browse . . .

13 The weather

Name

We don't usually like weather like this

We tend to prefer weather which is more like this

Look out of the window and see what the weather is like. What was the forecast for today? You can find out by looking at the BBC weather web site:

www.bbc.co.uk/weather

and also the Met Office web site:

www.met-office.gov.uk/

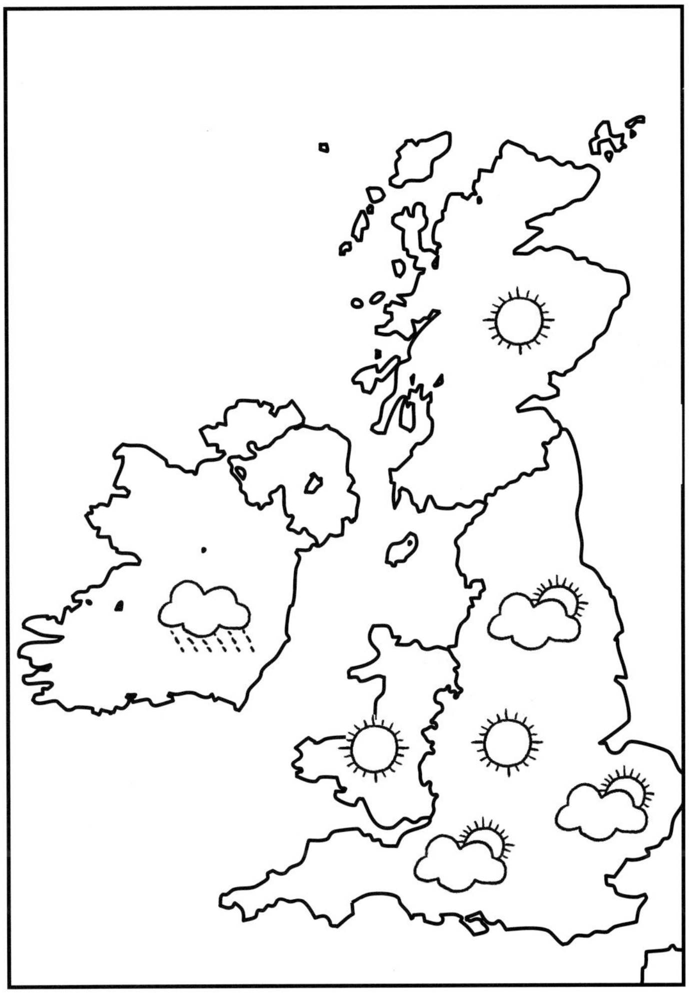

Is the weather the same for the whole country? What are the differences?
Go to '**regional**' and find out what the weather report said for your area.
Was the weather report correct?

Study the weather maps and see if you can predict the weather for tomorrow.
Download satellite images from the Internet.

Using the web sites for ideas, design your own weather chart. You need an outline of Britain and weather symbols which are easy to understand. (Or use ***My World*** weather screen to create your map.) Why not act being Sîan Lloyd or Michael Fish and present your weather forecast in front of a class? You could even record it on video!

Ask the infant class if they can understand what your symbols mean. You could turn it into a guessing game for them.

The Titanic

Name

New facts and figures are being found out about the *Titanic* all the time. Different evidence has already come to light since the recent film, about the way in which the *Titanic* sank.

From information you can find on the web site, construct a time-line of the events concerned with the sinking of the *Titanic*. Begin with the sighting of the iceberg and end with the sinking of the ship.

Web site: www.fireflyproductions.com/titanic/

From the web site information try to answer the following questions. Write your answers on the back of the sheet.

1 What year did the *Titanic* set out on her maiden voyage?

2 What type of passengers were on board?

3 Where was the ship sailing to?

4 What time was the iceberg sighted?

5 What warnings had the ship received about the icy conditions at sea?

6 What was the name of the Captain of the *Titanic*?

7 What was the name of the designer? Was he on board?

8 Find out three facts which contributed to the *Titanic* sinking.

9 Find out three reasons why so many passengers drowned.

10 Which ship rescued the survivors?

Illustrate your work by drawing a picture of the *Titanic*. Look at some of the pictures of the *Titanic*, find one you like and try to copy it.

Email a shadow

Name

Compare shadow lengths of a metre stick with those from another country.

You will need to take and record measurements on a sunny day at hourly intervals during the school day. Do this for a week. This will give you a good comparison.

You could do this at different times of the year, perhaps during the period covering the shortest and longest days. Why would a school in the southern hemisphere be good to work with?

Visit the IECC web site in order to see how other schools announce their projects.

www.iecc.org

1 Prepare your own message carefully, mentioning how long the project would last and what other things need to be taken into account e.g. start and finish time.

2 Email your proposed project to IECC inviting pupils across the world to help you with the project. Wait patiently for replies! Choose which schools to work with and email them. Also email the other schools thanking them for replying but saying that due to the response it was impossible to include all.

S P 3 Save and print out the data they send. Construct a graph to represent the two sets of data (or more sets if you have more than one other school).

4 Design and create a wall display on your work for others to read and enjoy.

Browse . . .

16 Religions of the world

Name

There are many different religions in the world today. Find out from the other pupils in your class which ones they know about.

Prepare a short talk on one of the main religions of the world: Christianity, Hinduism, Sikhism, Judaism, Islam, Buddhism.

Choose one which interests you.

Go to the following web site

www.theresite.org.uk

to find some of the answers to the following questions:

Where/when did the religion begin?

What is the name of the holy book?

What deity (god/goddess) is worshipped?

What is the name of the building used for worship?

What are the main festivals celebrated?

What type of food is eaten during festivals?

Are special clothes are worn?

Are there any special symbols or art associated with the religion?

Are music and dancing important to the religion?

You could use the computer and web site in your talk to help you to explain.

Browse . . .

17 Where do you live?

Name ....

Can you find where Britain is, on a map of the world?

Can you find the town where you live, on a map of Britain?

Can you find where your street or road is, on a town map?

Go to the following web sites and look at some maps of the area in which you live.

http://uk.multimap.com/map/places.cgi www.streetmap.co.uk/

Which web site shows you the clearest map? Why?

Can you find the major roads which run into your town?
What are the road numbers?

....

Is there a railway link? Where does the railway line go?

....

Is there a river which runs through or near your town? What is it called?

....

How far away is your nearest city? ....

Someone from your town wants to travel to the nearest city. On the back of this sheet write out a list of directions to get there by car. You should include road numbers and any villages they pass through. Also include places such as schools, hospitals, countryside, etc which they have to pass.

Without looking at any maps can you write a list of directions for your route to school from your home?

....

....

....

....

....

Car search

Name

You have just started working in a garage selling cars and a customer has asked you to find a secondhand Ford Escort built in 1994.

Use the following web sites to help you with your search:

www.exchangeandmart.co.uk www.autotrader.co.uk

Search for:

1 the cheapest **2** the dearest **3** the nearest

Compare using the online publication with the printed magazines (*Exchange and Mart* or *Autotrader*). What are the advantages and disadvantages of both?

Extension work:

You have to find some secondhand cars to stock your garage. Use the above web sites to choose 15 cars priced between £1,500 and £5,500 that could sell in your area. Record your results in a database using the following fields:

Make Model Colour Year Price cc Mileage

Represent the data collected as a bar chart. Print out your bar chart.

You could prepare your own questions for others to search your database.

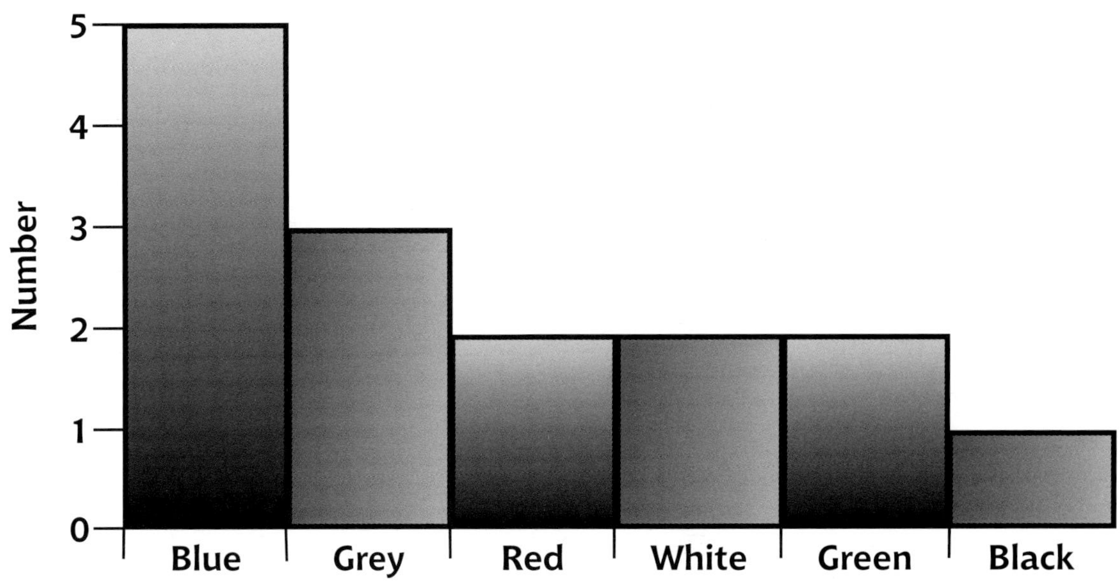

Browse . . .

19 Party time!

Name ______________________

It's your best friend's birthday.

You have been given the job of planning the party.

You have to find a **caterer** who will prepare the food.

You have to find an **entertainer** or D.J. to provide the entertainment.

You have to find a cleaning firm to clean the house after the party! Try searching for **domestic services**.

Go to the following web site and choose the businesses you think will meet your requirements.

www.yell.co.uk

Fill in the form below. This will help you to organise the arrangements.

Address of party

Date of party

Time of party

How many guests

Caterer – name and phone no.

Entertainer – name and phone no.

Cleaner – name and phone no.

Extension work:
Design an invitation card to send to all those invited.

Browse . . .

20 An assembly

Name ______________________________

Write an assembly for your class to perform. It can be about either

a) a world religion or **b)** an ethical or moral issue.

There is information on the following site:

http://re-xs.ucsm.ac.uk/

Things to consider:

1 Make sure that all the pupils in your class are involved.

2 Think about all the different religions in your school as a whole.

3 Ask your teacher for a time limit and work within that.

4 Keep it as simple as possible!

5 Choose hymns/songs that everybody knows!

6 Visit the newspaper sites for ideas for prayers (see Worksheet 1).

Start by writing a programme of events, making sure it fits the time scale.

Make a list of the things each pupil or groups of pupils have to do.

Prepare a script for those involved to follow.

Browse . . .

Dinosaur data

Name

There were many different types of dinosaur. Some were herbivorous, some were carnivorous. Some could fly, some walked on four legs. Some were very big, some were very small.

Go to the Natural History Museum web site: www.nhm.ac.uk

Click on ***Interactive***, scroll down and click on ***Dinosaur Data Files***. Find out just how many dinosaurs were in each of the following categories.

Fill in the chart below with your findings. Think of some other groupings and find out how many dinosaurs there are in those groups.

Dinosaur groups	How many
Herbivorous dinosaurs	
Carnivorous dinosaurs	
Flying dinosaurs	
Walked on two legs	
Walked on four legs	
Dinosaurs under 3 m high	
Dinosaurs over 3 m high	

Tip: In order to help you with your work you could print all the files on the different dinosaurs, create a database using the information or download the spreadsheet file and use it in Excel.

Extension work:
Click on ***some suggestions for activities*** found on the ***Dinosaur data files*** page and try some of the ***Classroom Activities***: **Creative writing** – Dinosaur names and A day in the life of...; **Size and scale** – Ordering, Pacing out, Scale models; **Sorting and comparing dinosaur data** – Challenge game.

S P Save and print some of the dinosaur pictures in ***The Online Picture Library***, which is found on the Museum's Home Page (i.e. first page).

Browse . . .

22 What's their web site like?

Name

Who is your favourite singer or band?

From the list of web sites below choose one band and review their web site.

www.boyzone.co.uk

www.backstreetboys.com

www.westlife.co.uk

Use the following questions to help you.

1 Is the web site colourful? ....

2 Does it give information on members of the band? ....

3 Are there pictures of the band? ....

4 Does it tell you what the band is doing at the moment? ....

5 Does it give you sound bites of the music? ....

6 Does it give you the words of the songs? ....

7 Does it let you email the band? ....

8 Does it let you join their fan club? ....

9 Is the web site easy to use? ....

10 How could the web site be better? ....

(You may need to ask your teacher permission to install Flash 4.0 to access the Backstreet Boys web site.)

Have a look at another band's web site from the list and see which site you like best. Why is it better?

Write up your findings and present your review to the rest of the class. Have the web site on the computer behind you as you talk to illustrate what you say.

Try to find the web site of your favourite singer. Use a search engine such as Yahoo or Alta Vista to find the site.

Browse . . .

23 Create a school web page

Name ______________________

You have been given the task of designing a school web page.

Here are some of the things you need to consider.

- It has to be informative and interesting to look at, for other pupils as well as adults wanting information about the school.
- You could include a jokes page which you could update each month.
- You could ask for new jokes to be emailed to you for inclusion.
- You could run a poetry competition each term.
- You could include your school email address.

The following web sites have some useful tips and links to school web pages that could give you extra ideas.

www.textease.com

www.sutton.lincs.sch.uk/tes

www.tes.co.uk

www.becta.org.uk

Present your findings to the class, ask them for their ideas and design a final draft.

When you do submit your web page, don't forget to advertise it! You can 'carbon copy' an email to other schools listed at www.iecc.org

Browse . . .

24 CD-Roms

Name

You have been given £200 to purchase CD-Roms for Key Stage 1 pupils and a further £200 to purchase CD-Roms for Key Stage 2 pupils.

Discuss in a group, and ask other pupils and staff what type of CD-Roms are needed for the different key stages. Make a list of the different types needed.

Use the following web sites to search for the different types needed and their cost:

www.becta.org.uk (CD reviews)
www.sherston.com
www.prodplay.com/

Search software catalogues in school for similar information.

Using both methods of searching for information, fill in the table below.

CD Title	Key Stage	Subject/Theme	Cost

From your list of CD-Roms for both age groups make a final recommendation to your class teacher, giving reasons for your decisions.

Compare using the online publication with the magazine you found. What are the advantages and disadvantages of both?

You could consider designing a spreadsheet to present your information.

25 Pupil's record sheet

Name .... **Date** ....

Activity ....

Web sites used ....

Software used ....

What I did ....

....

....

....

....

....

What I learnt ....

....

....

....

....

....

I found this activity . . . (circle appropriate words)

hard	**easy**	**fun**	**enjoyable**	**frustrating**
boring	**challenging**	**interesting**	**exciting**	

The Evans Brothers Bookshelf Collection

Title	ISBN
Dinosaurs KS1	0 237 51505 9
Food KS1	0 237 51579 2
Fun With Words KS1	0 237 51574 1
Library Skills KS1	0 237 51872 4
Library Skills KS2	0 237 51576 8
Making Books KS1/2	0 237 52001 X
Map Skills KS1	0 237 51767 1
Map Skills KS2	0 237 51768 X
Maths Outside KS1	0 237 51499 0
Maths Outside KS2	0 237 51500 8
Me and My Body KS1	0 237 51580 6
More Fun With Words KS1	0 237 51575 X
Number Resources for Numeracy YR	0 237 52011 7
Number Resources for Numeracy Y1	0 237 52012 5
Number Resources for Numeracy Y2	0 237 52082 6
Number Resources for Numeracy Y3	0 237 52083 4
Number Resources for Numeracy Y4	0 237 52084 2
Number Resources for Numeracy Y5	0 237 52085 0
Number Resources for Numeracy Y6	0 237 52086 9
Problem Solving Games KS1	0 237 51577 6
Problem Solving Games KS2	0 237 51578 4
Reading and Responding KS1	0 237 51581 4
Reading and Responding KS2	0 237 51582 2
Responding to Traditional Tales KS1	0 237 51497 4
Responding to Traditional Tales KS2	0 237 51498 2
Science Activities KS1	0 237 51501 6
Science Activities KS2	0 237 51502 4
The Sea KS1	0 237 51506 7
Using I.T. in Design and Technology	0 237 51816 3
Using I.T. in English	0 237 51813 9
Using I.T. in Geography	0 237 51818 X
Using I.T. in History	0 237 51817 1
Using I.C.T. in Internet Projects	0 237 52065 6
Using I.T. in Maths	0 237 51814 7
Using I.T. in Science	0 237 51815 5
Writing Skills KS2	0 237 51573 3

For further information please contact:

Sales Department
Evans Brothers Limited
FREEPOST 1
London W1E 2EZ

Tel: 0207 935 7160
Fax: 0207 487 5034

Glossary

CD-ROM (Compact Disc Read-Only Memory) A compact disc which can store a huge amount of data.

Cell A cell is a box found on a spreadsheet grid. A cell is located by its column letter and row number. Information can be entered into cells in the form of text or numbers.

Copy and Paste A facility that allows data to be duplicated and placed elsewhere.

Data Information that is entered into or produced by a computer. The data may be in the form of numbers, text, graphics or sounds.

Database An organised store of information.

Email Electronic mail which is sent using a computer

Field A heading used on a record in a database.

Formulae Mathematical equations which can be used in a spreadsheet to carry out calculations.

Internet The international network of computers linked to share information.

Online The status of a computer whilst connected to the Internet.

Record A 'page' of information entered into a database program.

Software Programs for a computer.

Spreadsheet A grid of cells. Data can be entered into these cells and then calculations performed on that data by using formulae.

Web page A screen of text and or graphics which is available to access through the Internet.

Web site Several web pages which are linked to create a whole.

Word processing A term used to describe the process of entering, storing and revising text.

Word processor A term used for a system using a word processing program.